Dear Parent:
Your child's love of reading starts here!

Every child learns to read in a different way and at his or her own speed. Some go back and forth between reading levels and read favorite books again and again. Others read through each level in order. You can help your young reader improve and become more confident by encouraging his or her own interests and abilities. From books your child reads with you to the first books he or she reads alone, there are I Can Read Books for every stage of reading:

SHARED READING
Basic language, word repetition, and whimsical illustrations, ideal for sharing with your emergent reader

BEGINNING READING
Short sentences, familiar words, and simple concepts for children eager to read on their own

READING WITH HELP
Engaging stories, longer sentences, and language play for developing readers

READING ALONE
Complex plots, challenging vocabulary, and high-interest topics for the independent reader

I Can Read Books have introduced children to the joy of reading since 1957. Featuring award-winning authors and illustrators and a fabulous cast of beloved characters, I Can Read Books set the standard for beginning readers.

A lifetime of discovery begins with the magical words **"I Can Read!"**

Visit www.icanread.com for information on enriching your child's reading experience.

Visit www.zonderkidz.com/icanread for more faith-based I Can Read! titles from Zonderkidz.

Lord, you have made so many things!
How wise you were when you made all of them!
The earth is full of your creatures.
—*Psalm 104:23–25*

ZONDERKIDZ

Cats, Dogs, Hamsters, and Horses
Copyright © 2010 by Zonderkidz

An **I Can Read Book**

Requests for information should be addressed to:

Zonderkidz, *3900 Sparks Drive SE, Grand Rapids, Michigan 49546*

Library of Congress Cataloging-in-Publication Data

Cats, dogs, hamsters, and horses.
    p. cm. — (I can read!)
        ISBN 978-0-310-72009-6 (softcover)
    1. Pets—Religious aspects—Christianity—Juvenile literature.
BT746.C38 2010
231.7'65—dc22   2009048440

All Scripture quotations, unless otherwise indicated, are taken from The Holy Bible, *New International Version®, NIV®.* Copyright © 1973, 1978, 1984, 2011 by Biblica, Inc.® Used by permission of Zondervan. All rights reserved worldwide. www.Zondervan.com. The "NIV" and "New International Version" are trademarks registered in the United States Patent and Trademark Office by Biblica, Inc.®

Any internet addresses (websites, blogs, etc.) and telephone numbers in this book are offered as a resource. They are not intended in any way to be or imply an endorsement by Zondervan, nor does Zondervan vouch for the content of these sites and numbers for the life of this book.

No part of this publication may be reproduced, stored in a retrieval system, or transmitted in any form or by any means — electronic, mechanical, photocopy, recording, or any other — except for brief quotations in printed reviews, without the prior permission of the publisher.

Zonderkidz is a trademark of Zondervan.

I Can Read® and I Can Read Book® are trademarks of HarperCollins Publishers.

Editor: Mary Hassinger
Art direction & design: Sarah Molegraaf

Printed in China

22 23 24 /DSC/ 12 11 10

··· MADE·BY·GOD ···

Cats, Dogs, Hamsters, and Horses

CONTENTS

Cats 5

Dogs 12

Hamsters 19

Horses 26

God made all animals.

Some animals

have become friends for people.

One special animal pet is called a…

CAT!

God made about forty different
kinds of cats.
Some are called Persian and Siamese.
Cats have different characteristics.
Persians have long, flowing coats
and flat faces.
Siamese have creamy-colored short
coats with darker ears, paws, and tails.
All cats have strong teeth and jaws,
good hearing, and can see well

Most cats live ten to fifteen years.
To keep a cat happy and healthy
people feed them a good diet
with vitamins and minerals.
Cats like to drink water.
People think milk is a good drink
for cats. But be careful!
Many cats get sick
if they drink cow's milk.

Cats need doctor visits just like people. But cats help take care of themselves too. They clean their fur by licking. Cats use their tongues, which feel like sandpaper, to do this job.

Cats let people know how they feel.
When cats are happy, they purr.
When cats are upset, they hiss
and can scratch.
If a cat gets nervous, you might
see its tail or ears twitch.

Cats love to play.

Cats like yarn, bells, and catnip.

They also like to just be petted.

God made all animals.

Some animals

have become friends for people.

One special animal pet is called a…

DOG!

Many people have dogs as pets. God made many breeds of dogs—so many that it is difficult to count. Some kinds of dogs are Labradors and Chihuahuas.

Some dogs make good friends for families.
These dogs are taught to be gentle and behave well.
They can be protective and love to run and play.

Some dogs learn special skills.
They help people live safely
and do their jobs.
Some dogs help people who cannot
see or hear well.
Other dogs help police find
lost people or things.

People who have dogs feed them diets with vitamins and minerals. Some dogs love to share people food, but it is not always healthy!

People can train their dogs

to do tricks.

Some people take their dog to school.

But don't forget, dogs love to

play too!

God made all animals.

Some animals

have become friends for people.

One special animal pet is called a…

HAMSTER!

God made many kinds of hamsters. Some hamsters that make good pets are Dwarf, Teddy Bear, and Panda hamsters.
These can all be found at pet shops along with supplies they need to stay healthy and safe.

Hamsters have poor eyesight.
Since many live in burrows,
it is fine for them.
Even if hamsters live in cages
they like to burrow under
torn-up paper and cardboard tubes.
Hamsters have good hearing, and
their noses work great too.

People keep their pet hamsters healthy with good food and fresh water. If they get sick, a veterinarian can care for a hamster.

To help a hamster stay healthy, people make sure the hamster has a clean cage and an exercise wheel for running. People even get clear exercise balls for their hamster to roll and ride in.

Hamsters have large front teeth that keep growing. They must have things to chew on, like hamster-safe sticks and even dog biscuits. These help their teeth stay short.

God made all animals.

Some animals

have become friends for people.

One special animal pet is called a…

HORSE!

There are more than 300 breeds of horses in the world. God made every one! People had horses before Jesus was born, more than 3,000 years before. There are cave drawings and bones in museums to show us.

People used horses for work and transportation long ago. Farmers used horses to plow or ride. Others used horses to pull carriages. Today, people have horses for work and enjoyment.

People who have horses feed them foods with vitamins and minerals, like oats, hay, and special grains. Some horses get treats like sugar and apples. Horses need lots of water every day.

Horses let their owners know how they feel.
The way a horse moves its body can show whether it is happy, upset, or scared and startled.

A horse will be a happy pet as long as its owner cares for and loves it, grooms and feeds it, and makes sure it has plenty of exercise and rest.